GHOSTS
and other company

JENNY JOSEPH

BLOODAXE BOOKS

Copyright © Jenny Joseph 1995

ISBN: 1 85224 295 7

First published 1995 by
Bloodaxe Books Ltd,
P.O. Box 1SN,
Newcastle upon Tyne NE99 1SN.

Bloodaxe Books Ltd acknowledges
the financial assistance of Northern Arts.

Cover printing by J. Thomson Colour Printers Ltd, Glasgow.

Printed in Great Britain by
Cromwell Press Ltd, Broughton Gifford, Melksham, Wiltshire.

GHOSTS AND OTHER COMPANY

to my friend Maja

Acknowledgements

Acknowledgements are due to the editors of the following publications in which some of these poems first appeared: *Aquarius, Encounter, European Judaism, The Forward Book of Poetry* (Forward Publishing, 1995), *The Listener, Memorials* (Ravette, 1986), *New Statesman & Society, Partisan Review* (USA), *P.E.N. Broadsheet, P.E.N. New Poetry* (Quartet, 1986), *Poetry Book Society Anthology 1987-88* and *1988-89* (PBS/Hutchinson, 1987 & 1988), *Poetry Review, The Rialto, The Scotsman,* and *With a Poet's Eye* (Tate Gallery Publications, 1986).

'The allotted time' was included in an earlier collection by Jenny Joseph, *The Thinking Heart* (Secker & Warburg, 1978). 'Delayed crossing' was published in a memorial volume for Alan Hancox edited by Alan Tucker and published by the Whittington Press. 'In a dark stone' was commissioned by Central Productions for the *Talk, Write...and Read* Teachers' Notes, and 'By Lake Huron' on a Friends of the Cheltenham Festival of Literature poster. 'Expecting guests' was broadcast on *Poetry Now* (BBC Radio 3).

Contents

The allotted time

The allotted time for the return of ghosts
Is it plotted
Along a graph of time; as on a map
The place to meet is here where two roads cross
Or there by the station incline?

The blood spattered on the lorry head
The mud
Tossed up when the cab ploughed its windscreen through the ditch
Marks for succeeding years the accident
The lorry moves under.

Is there some substance behind bright circles
In the air
Staring eyes that look in the light can make –
Thickening breath, or shapes against the sky
To warn us in time?

You cannot by longing make a ghost appear,
Nor by forethought
Force him not to. I can or needn't go
To the roadside meeting, but how can we avoid
Junctions in time?

We move on a road jammed by moments
That follow us.
Others pursue and hound us along our route.
When from the swirling black of the fields at the side,
Stood in the headlights,

Appear – pleading, luring, dementing,
Too near –
The gestures of a figure, oh covey of ghosts
How can I give your representative due welcome?
You've no real kingdom.

If I make obeisance to you and lead off the road
Over the bank
I shall wake only in the charred sticks of the dead,
Not the faint palaces that sometimes seem
Clearer than earth I tread.

I

A chair in my house, after Gwen John

The house is very still and it is very quiet.
The chair stands in the hall: lines on the air;
Bar back, a plane of wood, focus in a space
Polished by dusk and people who might sit there.

Pieces of matter have made it. To get in words
What you could do in paint
Only the simplest sentences will serve.

And in this presence how much "elsewhere" lurks.
It is a sort of listening to the air
That laps the object, a breathing in of light
That's needed if we are to see the chair.

Here I pare this little stick of words
To keep away the crowds
And set my chair down, which words can never do.

The yellow daisies clash in the wind outside
It's not for long we can ignore they're there
Your noisy letters are dead in a box in the town
Your pictures breathe this wordless atmosphere.

The day goes through the room: dusk, white wall, through
To dusk again, and my wooden chair stands there.
I cannot get my chair the way you do
The things you paint.
Even the simplest sentence will not do.

Trompe l'œil

Old woman
Sitting by the fire
Making a lap from spread legs, and the scarfed outline
Of the little old body in the picture books;
Veined hand forcefully on knee to heave you up
From mental dawdlings mulling by the fire
In order to fetch something, to laugh, to make a rough crack,
Tough enough as old boots are to be capacious
For the lumpy foot that can fit none of the shoes
On offer in the shops; –
Stop being busy and practical for a minute,
Turn your head.
I've blown the cover you use for every day.
You can bring out now the small child from the folds
Of the air where you've hidden her about your person.
She is rising through the palimpsest
Of the way you lean and look and scramble up,
As a shadow strengthens at the strengthening sun.
There's still this young fruit, this kernel, this shape in little
From which the tree has grown,
Not child of your womb, or child's child that, separating,
Continued your life elsewhere, but – ghost if you like,
Pattern within the substance,   rings of a tree
Still living in the wood for the eightieth year
To be there too.

You have withdrawn to look for something to show me
Leaving me in the company of a small bright child
Sitting by the fire heaving its cat in its arms.

A glimpse in a lay-by

I see an old man's hand
Quivering, as the edge of my sandwich wavers
And drops to the car seat I'm leaning across to get it:
It's beyond his grasp to hook into his mouth.
I see him walking at an angle, tense
Quick and eager, jerky, carrying cases.
I see the hand as old not because
I thought of him as old then, but because now
I see myself as such, and my hand
And the awkward stoop of my head to catch the crumbs
As I bent sideways from the steering wheel,
Parked in some nameless lay-by on one of those journeys
He must have done a thousand times,
Was my father's.

November returns

Firework time; and this year, gales.
Large trees dip and bow tearing their leaves
Against the air, which seems to thicken now.
Not a quiet time even when the weather is quiet.
Fireworks, and your birthday: the year beginning
Apart from the calendar. A time when things have happened.
Advenire, Advent: to come to reach to happen.

Some years there is sunshine pale in woods.
It lies in splashes like paint on leaves, on the track,
A pausing in the year before it swings
Down to the dark,
And the leaves thin – beech-gold, pebble-brown –
A clearing in the grove.
On some dim soft dun afternoon
Having to wait for something, you go a stroll
At the back of the Works ('back in twenty minutes').
An astounding tree picked out by secret sunshine
Makes sense of the Golden Bough, the magic in woods.

Bonfires, Hallowe'en past, children running through streets,
Something stirring in the blood that makes us rise
And stand at the window, leaving the curtain ajar,
Expectant of something, watching, waiting
For something to happen; someone, perhaps, to arrive.
Maybe it is just the wind shifting direction
Dropping leaves at doors, pattering rain on the windows.

I draw the curtains, light the fire, for you
And others I have lit for at this time:
Ghosts returning to their winter quarters
To keep me company, to celebrate the season.

Come and have dinner

Come and have dinner, ghosts, you would be welcome
You who are really dead, and you wraiths, who,
Gone from my life are having proper dinner
In the flesh, of flesh, elsewhere; and to whom
I may not even be a memory.

When people are together there are battles:
Needs, exactions, hopes. Returns are looked for
On all the thought we lavish, for lives given over.

More easily than those times, I bid you welcome.
Come smiling, in good spirits; leave behind
Cantankerous habits, the tetchiness that deflates
Balloons of generosity. Restrain your grudging
And longings to be elsewhere, as I will do.

The food will be better too. Unembarrassed
By any real demands, failings or pain,
Incapable of all those wants that lean
On live association, you've no better chance now
Than what I make of you. Let us encourage
A memory that is at home here, a habit of presence.
Without misplacing the contents, you can inhabit
The absences in this house, and join the mesh
Holding the years that travel through its fabric.

Come and dine, ghosts. We could say
It is a birthday and you the bidden guests
Though I need no excuses to get at your company now.

Unfinished business makes a ghost they say.
Since actions did not balance expectations,
The bridge from each side missing in the middle
Unfinished,   I wonder

Whether even out of life, your ghost returning
Could find the right place yet?
A bridge, the transoms passing at the centre,
Is just the gap for ghosts to come to:
(The 'Monsieurs' and 'Mesdames' of the song still dance
Still dance in a round on the butt ends at Avignon.)

There'll always be enough unsatisfactory,
Enough undone, for a small gap to open,
(A warped window-sill never quite flush with the wall)
And sometimes, the conjuring of your fading presence
Levers it a little and gives you passage.

Dinner is ready, the room is cleaned and warm.

Be my guest.

In honour of love

In your honour I have cleaned the windows
Of four-months' sorrow-flung obscuration and dirt
And cut my hair and thrown away old rags
That make cupboards foetid, suffused with miserly pain.
I shall wipe the mould out of the corners
Rub down, prepare to paint;   in your honour.

And in your honour
Am throwing out old nastiness with the floorboards,
Memories of hurt, lese-majesty
Along with the shards and glue, useless and hard now.

As if for new love turning a new leaf over
I will pick off infestation up to the minute.
At this time of budding give a chance to cleanliness
Make beds freshly in garden, and in the house
Fresh covers; as if with hope square corners
In expectation, in honour of your coming.

For your comfort and in your honour
I have laid by stores and funds of robustness
Sweeping despondence out with the spiders' coatings
Disinfecting anxiety, self-pity
The damp that clads, sours and eats the woodwork.

I think it isn't true that ghosts return
Only to ruins and to broken things.
Shy visitants that start to come with me
Along the track I make you from the past
By thinking of you, you would never bear
Burdens you could not shoulder when alive.
You'll still want cheering, self-reliance, comfort
The big wheel pulling up the hill, hearth cleared,
Coal ordered, landlord dealt with, 'sociables',
And so to welcome you and keep a place
For your reviving influence to bide in
I move within the chrysalis of doubt
Wound round for winter comfort, for survival.

In honour of love, in hope of expectation
I leave behind drab covering that kept me
Safe through the winter, safe and solitary.

The grub without its carapace is needed
Pale and soft and vulnerable, for birds
Shining and voracious.   So,
I am persuaded, every time a fool.
Well, something must feed the remorselessness of spring.

The skin will burst, so you should see light wings
No dirty brown slough. The bad times swept away,
Place ready for the prodigal,
                                        and be damned the peril
The piercing light and the brief high flight will bring.

Ashes, when you have gone, burnt bits on the lamp
That lit you on your way, but in your honour
As you pass by the window, love, – bright flame.

Delayed crossing

(for Alan Hancox)

Spring rain is falling
The sky pulls back even through the rain
To lengthen the evening.
Soft quiet rain and the ghosts gather
Gather to sip and release their susurrations
Across the courtyard, round the house, at windows
Through gurglings in gutters, through tricklings of spring rain.

They ebb and flow
As gnats that sway at dusk. Refreshed they come
To freshen our minds.
Beneficent, these our ghosts, visiting
Filling our lack, friends who have recently died
And joined each other in our memories
As separate drops fill up a hole in the gravel.

Their breath is silk
With gentle sad gestures they soften hard hurting thoughts;
Modest, wary
They gather in diffident concourse; attending.
But you have not come with them in the grey.
You have not reached the shadowed world, the edges.
You have not retired to coverts to wait for evening.

Through Cheltenham's day
Tough in the sun so solidly you stride.
You stand and talk
And cook and serve and greet. You smile:
The print is full colour still, no negative's shading.
You wave goodbye as you go off on some errand.
It will be a long time till you join the shadows.

A letter

Dear Friends,

                Winter has come here.
It is not too bad as yet, though the darkness
Takes the centre, takes over, is beginning to make
Other things vague and futile.   It
Is not all bad;   the trees
Are sometimes very beautiful, it's just
It's sad that summer has left us. It's more difficult
To get done the things expected of us. That apart
It suits me in a way.   Perhaps
The slowness of the blood begins to suit me.
It lets you out – winter – and I feel so lazy.
What can you do but let things go, in winter?

I write these things to you in another country
Lest in fine weather you should sorrow for me
And wish me in another place. I soon will be;
Like you in a climate untouched by the seasons
Except in people's minds. The dead are unreached
By any of our changes and yet we think
Of you as minding that we think of you,
As bathed in sunlight, comforted by air.
I write to you, dear Friends, to let you know
That I am all right here, knowing often
Love and glad things I wouldn't have elsewhere
But turning, really, longing sometimes so strong
For my quittance, my papers, my number to come up
And set off for your country.

                    See you soon.

Generation gap

'Where have you been, child, that took so long in coming?'
'Curled up in a warm place with the other animals.'

'Why did you not come sooner, while I could play with you?'
'My mother was playing, and had no time for me;

But you could have seen to the living. They had need of you.
If I were with you now I'd cry and be annoying.
You'd wish for peace again.'

'It is true, my twinkle, my apple of the eye,
That when you are born you will be wet and squally
And when you are growing I shall worry and complain.
But dreams are fed, my darling, on messy living beings.
It's contrary old people who have no use for pallor:
They want the sun, and comfort and real soft flesh again.

All that time you kept off when I could have been with you
Were you somewhere gathering merit, becoming beautiful?'

'Curled up in your mind, grandparent, keeping you company
And better there, I reckon, than a brat on this bothersome earth.'

Expecting guests

I have made a seat in the yard
I have clipped the hedge and swept out the corner
Of crinkly plastic pots, split, whose plants
Long since ceased to come to anything.

I have made a seat in the yard.
It is not a proper do-it-yourself shop one
But the seat and back of a broken chair I did not burn
Set level on some bricks I found by the path.
There's serendipity for you, a thing made
Out of things found, much the same as you are.

It is high enough for very short legs only.
Too low, this seat, for anything but small squatters.
When will you come and visit me, arrival?
You will like it here in your place that just happened
One happy day;
From chancy rubbish: an aimed arrangement.

You, floating past creeks, promontories, islands
Chancily washed into the flowing current
That is bringing you this landfall after all,
Visitant from the unmarked stuff that stretches
In every direction round our patch, where things
Become visible like the circle a lamp furnishes
Viewed from the dark,
Friend from the other side, before and after,
When, season's bird, will you come, alight
Matching your landing to the swaying branches,
Come and lighten, sunshine, the corner I have made you
And where I await you?

Patriotic poem against nationalism
for a newborn child

1

Is it too bright for you, darling?
Under the yews in the churchyard
Inland from the town, into the hills, up the lanes
It is cool and green-shadowed and quiet;   and there

LYETH the Bodi of Ann David
Who died the 21st January 1784
Aged one month – so born just about Christmas.
And you are two days, born into flaming June.

2

Many the infant children buried here
Beneath elaborate tiles, and graved slate
Polished hard and clean with the lettering
As clear as the day it was done.

Memorials, important, memories solid
For each little scrap of throw-away life
Slate thick and heavy as marble, but dimmer
And, absorbing the light, seeming more part of the earth.
The hillside sleeps in the morning sun, in the years
Of sleep that has come to this place.
Beyond the shaded porch-path, out in the field
Light pours unwinking on the bright new graves.

3

'Genth' I shall call you, who have no Welsh in you.
Little Welsh girl, little scrap born in Wales.
We have no Welsh in us, and I no drop of Celtic.
But I more than you likely to learn these stones
And I, for no reason, more likely to learn this language.

4

To the traveller
Any place they come to can be home
Even for a day or two
And any language learnt can be our own
For as long as we care to use it, can be
In that we all are strangers somewhere.
Everything we know
We have to learn, even what we are,
Become the part we practise.

You come from wandering people much attached
To places here and there, and fed by roots
(What that lives isn't?) but like water lilies
Floating in moving streams
That take and give back wherever they find themselves;
            from people attached to the day
Wherever it fades or opens. The same light
Flowing round somewhere else will make you blink,
As you do now, gossamer, so frail, so silken,
Force you to come to terms, force you to stir.

5

Later you will get
Particulars: names nationalities opinions,
A history, and be pulled along the track
Your people make to travel on.
                                        Now
It is just life and air and the June sun
Shining by the sea on Wales,
A morsel of flesh and its light breathing,
Gossamer-light for life, durable,
Tough as thistle-down or the fair hair of the dandelions
Seeding to make the inextirpable roots
That fill the banks with flowers.

6

I drive from dark shadows up into light again
The sun hitting my mirror
Plunged into dazzle of darkness I continue half blind
Until sight settles.
We swing from dark to light to dark, swaying
Between the Poles
We clutch, we scream   and you, tiny slip,
Take it all so quietly. You are so calm
Blinking, adjusting, your blood settling no doubt
To pulse at its own speed now, in its separate world.
It has been dark where you have come from
Dark and quiet like the churchyard on the hill
Drowsing in noontide, dark surrounded by light.

7

Too much is put on children by our wishes:
To carry the banner, to forge and protect the nation,
To make Utopia, which we could not do.
We really should not wish you anything
Except good luck and health and the wit to use them.
But – old ritualist – I want my wishes.
I wish you may
Avoid being mired by the past or the claim of sects;
Not lose the sense of history, but loose
The clutch of the bitter ghosts unsettled people
Feed with acrid blood, as some keep dogs
Hungry on the highway.
It is for such as you who everywhere
Turn to their mother's milk, try out the air,
Move away from the glare, that if we could
We would change nations into geography.

I hope you will love whatever place you live in
Because you love it, not because commanded
By joyless people gritting their teeth for power;
Welcomed everywhere, and safe enough
To welcome others and like them for their strangeness.
This is for later,
                                            for now
Welcome, strange darling, into this new place
Where you have lighted, soft and quiet as thistledown
To thrive wherever you land, Madog, my girl from Wales.

Skipping song

circular chain

Listen to the air
Hush babe
Let me listen
Listen to the thought in me
Babe in me

The edge of the circle flames with light
Hide babe
Like the after-image of a burning ring
Come babe
Mercury, fire that does not burn
Babe in me

Do not
Break the circle
Interrupt the beat
Or stop listening

The stone
Makes the ripple
Makes the circle

The movement
Turns the rope
Turns the air
In a circle
Dazzles on the air

The movement
Breaks the circle
The stone
Breaks the water

After-image of the circle of light
(Do not stop do not burn)
Child.
Child in me
Lean and listen
Do not interrupt
Child, thought in me
As you turn the rope
Move your arm
Make the arc thresh
(Again and again
Thwack thwack on the ground)
Don't stop, whirl it round
Make the arc whirl
Or the rope falters, coils
Dead snake, a dead snake
Dead rope on the ground.

Lean and listen, rapt
Do not interrupt
Child
Keep the circle
Flaming.

In a dark stone

'About 7000 thousand years ago
There was a little girl
Who looked in a mirror
And thought herself pretty.'

'I don't believe you. All that time ago
If there was a little girl she'd be wild
Wearing skins, and living in damp woods.'

'But 7000 years ago
When England was a swamp with no one in it,
Long before the Romans,
In other lands by rivers and in plains
People made necklaces and learnt to write
And wrote down their accounts, and made fine pots,
Maps of the stars to sail by, and built cities;
And that is where they found this mirror
Where once the Hittite people roamed and ruled.'

'So you were there, were you, all that time ago
And living far from home, in ancient Turkey?'

'No, but I saw this mirror. Here in England.
It was the smallest thing in a large hall
Of great bronze cauldrons, statues, slabs of stone.
You mustn't think that it was made of glass
Common, like our mirrors.
                                        It was
A little lump of stone, shining; black; deep;
Hard like a thick black diamond, but better: obsidian.
It would have fitted in the palm of your hand.
One side was shaped and polished, the back rough.
Small though it was I crossed the room to see it.

I wanted to look in it, to see if it worked
Really, as a mirror, but I waited.'

'Why did you wait till nobody was round you?
You weren't trying to steal it were you?'
                                        'No. I was scared.

I waited and came slowly to it sideways.
I put my hand in front. It worked as a mirror.

And then I looked into that polished stone.
I thought the shadow of the shape I looked at
Was looking out at me. My face went into
That dark deep stone and joined the other face
The pretty one that used to search her mirror
When she was alive thousands of years ago.

I don't think she'd have come if there'd been a crowd.
They were all looking at the gold and brass.'

'I wish I could see it. Would she come for me?'

'I think the mirror's back in Turkey now.'

'I'd travel miles and miles if I could see it.'

'Well, nearer home, there were flint mines in Norfolk
And just where the land slopes a bit above some trees
On the Suffolk-Norfolk border, there's a track
And once I saw... But that's another story.'

Afterwords

When I am not with you
Why, I may be on the Common;
I may be on the tube
On my way home with the throng.

When I'm no longer with you
I shall be the loser.
You must not feel a lack;
Your thoughts are always with me.
My life filled up with yours
Will come home with the others.

When I am not with you
And am no longer with you
After the long release
O, then I shall hear you singing.

Who knows but thoughts like birds
May settle down on you?
One day looking up
When January smells of spring
And a blackbird calls from dark air,
Feeling the sky full of movement,
Who knows but you may think:
'The thoughts of someone who loves us
Are moving up there'?

II

Ballad of Rodborough Common

High on Rodborough
(Listen to my tale)
Stands an empty house
Commanding the vale.

Deep in grass on Rodborough
Two lovers lay
Sleeping murmuring fondling
The hours away.

Heavy in forgetfulness
The man slept;
To her house half down the dell
The woman crept.

Dog rose and elder flower
Pushed gutter high;
A light thrown on her ruined yard
Stopped her cry.

She crawled like a thief to her own back door
Hugging the wall
Two people sat at her table talking:
She heard it all:

He dealt the cards 'What will you lay?'
'I've nothing left but my clothes,' she said.
'The clothes from off your back I'll play
Against my holy love,' he said.

He drew and won and had the clothes
As she took them off her back, and then
Fixing his shining eyes on hers
'I'll play you the light from your eyes,' he said.

She drew and gasped. He took her light.
'What else will you give for love?' he said.
'I've nothing left but the skin on my bones.'
'I'll play for the bloom off your skin,' he said.

He drew and laughed and took her skin
And put it away in a box all folded.
'Clothes off your back, light from your eyes, bloom off your skin-
What next?' he said.

'The only thing that I've got left
Is what you've had long since,' she said.
'I'll give the blood that seeps from my womb
To get the other things back,' she said.

He drew and won. He took the blood
'And now I'll have the heart,' he said.
'I'll give you the heart from my body again
If you'll give me yours in exchange,' she said.

'My heart is made of words,' he said
As he dealt the cards for one more spate
'If I give it to you there'll be nothing there
In air it will evaporate.'

He played for her heart and wrenched it out
Of its place in her body 'and now' he said
'What have you left to give for love?'
'There is only the peace of my limbs,' she said.

He took her peace, and anguished and faint
She made a last plea and she drew her last bid
'To get my own love back again
I'll play you the strings of my mind,' she said.

He played. He won. Got up to go
Leaving her slumped in the chair as dead;
Hand on the kitchen door he turned
Not really listening to what she said.

'Give me a piece of your mind in return
For all the life you've taken,' she said
'My mind is only a mirror made up
Of pieces out of yours,' he said.

'You have had the joy from my eyes,' she said.
'The bloom from my skin, the skin from my bones
The guts from my belly, the clothes from my back
The peace from my body, my heart from its rest
You have taken all these and thrown them away.
Are you giving me nothing back?' she said.

'Give me at least my mind again
Which you do not want, which you cannot use
That with it I can grow again
Skin, bloom, light, breath and get once more
All things thereto to make me live.
Give me back my sense again
To see and do the truth,' she said.

'That's not the way the game of love
Is played' he said. 'I did not play
With you' she said, 'and that you know.'
'Of course,' he said 'and that is why
I chose to play the game with you.'

The watching woman found her way
Sick and shaking to the place
They had picknicked and played and slept, and she saw
The man from their house in her lover's face.

The food she had brought him she let fall
And the cover to keep him from the night air
Shaking and sick she went over the hill
That sheltered the man still sleeping there.

Now elder stems grow
Through a broken chair
In a house standing empty
On Rodborough.

Old tale

They say that if a wolf, padding in the forest
Sees a man who is not looking at it
And stares at him, his power to speak will die;

But if he sees the beast before it rolls
Its yellow beam towards him, can use his speech
To throw the onslaught, and turn the hypnotic eye.

I was walking in a sunny clearing
And did not see the danger in the shadows.
Your glare has frozen the heart that could tell you why.

Not the usual reverse

Hear this tale, an old cliché:
The traveller goes down the path to the place bethought of
Pannier fixed to take back the treasure, pick
And shovel newly cleaned.

He finds the cave broke up and empty.
Death rears.

Now by some unaccountable illusion
This story is traced in the mirror land of that.
A figure goes down another track unmindful
Unaiming of adventure, and pausing only
To change shoes and eat a sandwich, finds itself
Sat beside a cave glittering with treasure
A feast prepared, attendance ready waiting.
From the rock's shadow where drinking water trickles
A strange spirit, surely not death, looms.

Who am I to persist in my journey, then,
When I could stop and drink?

The uninvited

What are all these uninvited guests doing
Swarming through my life, up my stairs
Telling me how badly I have done things
Using my stores, pushing away my furniture and carrying
Boxes they shoulder into the middle of my rooms, unpacking
Immoveable objects so I cannot get through doors.
Here they stand at every corner with lists of things to blame me with
Appearing in the street and stopping me from getting to work where
        others
Blame me for that. I weep in corners, oppressed.

The early morning is cold and wet and depressing.
I hardly dare move my timorous limbs for dread
I will bring some fresh disdain.
I listen to the rain
And as each real minute seeps in with it someone says:
They have all gone. The day is yours again.
I look round and it is so, and the voice is mine.
I wake, glad to be so, glad even of rain and cold
And work and dirt and gloom.
I am ready to praise anything, for oh Heaven,
That terrible gang has gone.

A call across the dark

Suddenly the fog shuts down
And makes this place into a town
Like ones I knew an age ago:
A blurry focus all aglow
Isolate in dark countryside.

Oh child, I've lost you in the murk.
None of the usual methods work
For finding our way back again
Across hills blotted out with rain
That drifts in with the estuary tide.

Thrown, I halt. I pray it's true
You know where you are going to
For I saw, as the fog came down
The perilous roads around the town;
The landslips, the chasms gaping wide.

It is my own life that I weep
In losing you, and vainly keep
The image of your eager face
Fixed in my lurching mind, in case
Doing so, spells might work again

And shining in the morning air
You stand in safety beaming there
Strong feet set on the well-pathed land,
With total trust reach out your hand
Looking up through subsiding rain.

This after all is *your* fairy tale
And may be, charmed, you'll cross the vale
That writhes in horrors now for me
Who once unscathed crossed land and sea
Kept close by the fog of ignorance

And leapt across the narrow pass
Blind to the abyss with innocence.

Song

'Prepare yourself for death,' the old man said
And I, being a child
Crossed arms upon my chest
And said goodbye.

'Prepare yourself for life,' the preacher said.
Obedient as a child
I opened the window wide
And the rain came in.

'Prepare yourself for nothing,' my memory said
'Emptiness, silence, if I look to you.'
I turned the handle on the door at last
And walked through.

Paper tigers paper loves

Draw me a cat to frighten mice
Write me a love that has no ending
Fashion a flower out of gold
Send me a swan chiselled from ice.

And I will provide you with clockwork mice
A box for the papers the attic can hold
A jeweller's flower-bed that doesn't need tending
And a fridge from my heart to keep the swan nice.

Marching song
in easy tempo

You march along with me
You whom I've known.
You come along with me
You, who are gone.

Not of course as ghost
As memory, as you were:
To come along with me
To take you in to the future
I make you as you are.

So march along with me
Your passport is my thought.
Better now our ease
Your friendship, your support

Than when you could have given
Me space in your baggage
But refused so sternly
To stow me in your steerage.

I have made out your papers
Practised your signature.
Here is a space I've saved
For your gestures and furniture.

I suppose I could take you along now,
Fill in a claim to a past,
You that I fashion into
New friend from old ghost.

Uncartography

People on opposite shores
Crossing, recrossing;
The ferries always passing.

Like the story of the corn fox and hen
We are moved alternately towards each other
But never left near our food by the ferryman.

My map says
The years slide by as these banks do.
Unconfirmed against the real land
Is the map of love.

I wonder
Do the ferries still cross that far water
And what shores,
What shore unmappable of mind
Does your love lap now?

A visit

The tulips down the garden path
Grow so straight
A guard of red and yellow soldiers
From the gate.

The tulips this May morning
Grow so tall
In the narrow space
Along the wall.

I have seen it forty years
Exact and clear
In my mind, and yesterday
I went to where

The gate, I thought, had opened
Through the wall,
And I had gone past tulips
Straight and tall.

A drab hut on a weedy patch
Had turned about.
I spent an hour or so bemused
Trying to work out

How I'd have gone through a gate
Which wasn't there
Holding my breath that morning
Up to the door.

Let us hope today's young
People will
Go on errands heart in mouth
Pounding still,

And keep for forty years
Some quivering light
Thrown off from a place where tulips
Grew so straight
Red and yellow soldiers
From the gate.

Piano practice exercises

Grey days grey days
Valley filled with mist
Brown trees empty trees
That once the sunlight kissed

Old dog finished dog
Slumped by the fire
Old man crippled man
Longing for desire

Now we climb the hill again
Through the evening rain
See again the lit-up town
Quivering on the plain

Some come up as we go on
Down the other side.
May they see the lights we know
Sparkling up the tide.

Dirge

You ask me not to write;
I quite see why.
You want no mourning:
I will not cry.

You want to hold the world
As you've always done
The way you think it should be,
Though it's gone.

Now you've relinquished
Even a ghostly eye
I write to you,
And I can cry.

Song

I put out my hand to the fruit of the tree
That has beckoned, that has said
'Come and pick me.'

A gathering has seeped through all the long year.
It has filled, it has coloured.
The time is here.

'Bring the long ladder so you can reach me.'
Through bushes, over grass I heave it
Under the tree,

Get a basket, use the hour for this.
'It has swelled, it has waited
Take the bliss.'

I reach out my hand to the fruit of the tree.
Up the great blue dome a bird flies high
Away from me.

The buried army at Xian

There have always been
Watchers in tombs
Slaves foxes thieves.
But do the dead still watch?

Through dusk of the day
I knew you were dying
A hedgehog emerged
On to grass I was watching
In the garden where I listened.
Dim hump where light was leaving.
The air was charged with portent.

The sand has drifted
Like drifts of cloud in sleep
A sleep of centuries

On some monuments
A beetle or a searching rat in stone:
Metempsychosis, or
The ravages of time.
Something escaping from the rot of flesh
The soul scurrying to next habitat?

Silent armies of the Emperor
Moving, cloth-shod, in twos and threes
    down passages
Converging for your last eternal duty
Phalanxes that gathered
Armed and in formation
Standing guard to warn the Emperor,
Your watch is eastward where the enemy
    comes from
Watching the night out, night of millenia

We have disturbed the sleep of the warriors
And made them stand upright,

As if
We were to plough the poppies in again
Trenching them back again into the earth
And make the revealed dead
Gather their limbs, settle their helmets on
Struggling upright in twos and threes in the ditches
(With here and there a fallen comrade leaning
As if asleep – on mud, or nestled on shoulder)
And stand to attention to salute the last post sounding

        Against the pull of the ground
        Their horizontal.

    Lay them down, lay them down
    Cover them over, unfix their staring eyes
        Let them rest.

I'm standing late at night
In an emptied part of the city.
A small-hours' gust sends smoke from a
    brazier
Over a pile of sand at a fenced-off roadworks.
From grit and fog and shivers of tiredness
    emerge
Outlines of figures, wisps from the pile of
    sand
Dispersing down vague alleys of the air:
One year, two thousand, coiling up from
    the past
Push through the cover of time into the
    present.
The dead and buried are keeping their
    watch on the living.

You who will never be a ghost
It is your voice in this life that I hear
Not from the past, but as if you telephoned.
Egypt, the North, Mathematics, the stars,
As food and fags and drink and your good body,
Were pleasures to you, and to your end
The swagger of a good looker made you shine.
Beam of generous love, your fulsome gifts
Re-commended the world, all your geese swans.

I wander round London, I think I hear the phone.
It is I who haunt, not you.

The next July
Keeping the date
Keeping that week of your death
I saw the hedgehog.
I stumbled over him on the dark path among the buckets
And then
Never again.

Later, outlines of a warm October,
Through mist in valleys and in towns;
Lights up before shops shut, people,
Busy through the dusk, and the night
Inhabitable, not a separate country
Beyond the limit of our circle of light.
Through it comes
The soft insistent breathings of Hallowe'en.
                    The time of return – not this year's dead though;
                    Not recent ghosts these waiting warriors

                    Waking from drifts
                    Drifts of sand

                    Drifts of clouded sleep
                    Sleep of centuries

                    Silent phalanxes
                    You stand waiting.
                    In Christian monuments
                    The Dead awaken
                    Bodies assemble, reassemble, gather
                    A silent troop,
                    An army gathers under the sand
                    Beavering in the night
                    Night of millenia.

Weak torso falling, soldier on brother soldier
Head on his shoulder falling, going, so tired
Falling into the long sleep, sleep of the centuries.

Now light has prised eyes open
Like a jemmy a coffin
Treasure to peer at
Prising out the meaning
Dust falls as you open your eyes
You flag, you fall, you crumble

Later we found the shard of an old hedgehog
Carrion cleaned, thrown on a dump, not smelling
Flexible spine mat, cleaned white-skin underside
Dead and much like a doormat, pink underneath.

Cohorts all tangled, the lines all out of
    order
Chariots overturned, horses
Pulling over the shafts
As their knees keeled and broke

Leave them so
Cover them over
Let them rest.

You sleep on your side as the wind un-
    covers you
Blowing the sand shallow, life and the air
    destroying
As death did not, your perfect pose and
    order

It is an accident that you remind us
Of a tombed knight awaiting resurrection;
And something your makers could not
    know, that the plain
Devoted to monument, riddled with
    guards of the dead,
Had living armies marching over your heads
Before the clay was dry.

The hedgehog comes into view from a place of darkness
And then is found on a dump chewed clean by insects.
Goodbye, my friend; but you believed in this life:
It is your voice I hear, and your love that keeps me.

The new day, unarmed, leaves no holes to hide in
The enemy has been gone for thousands of years
The East comes in scorchingly with its bold blank glare

A few *do's* and *don'ts* to help you care for your equipment

Give some attention to the face:
The fronting signboard of our lives and loves,
Starting position in the race.

Pay some attention to the hair:
Woman's glory, man's comfort,
Pulse of animal health gleams there.

Protect the vulnerable hands:
Agents of thought, tools
Intrinsic to the brain's commands.

Do not neglect your feet, for you
While you can walk
Depend on them to get you through.

Lift like a bowl your lungs, breathe in:
Only the pathways of the air
Supply you if you are to win.

Keep trim the ports and mechanisms
The eyes the ears the nose the skin
The portals where our *nous* homes in.

Tend the poor body as it's twirled
In time and space. It is
Your only gateway on the world.

'Birth copulation death'

T.S. Eliot's Sweeney

Wrap me up and hold me close
A baby needs to feel secure
Against the pressure of the light
Against the drumming threat of sound

 Loose my limbs and let me go
 Flinging, open to the sky
 All the air within my lungs
 Every land, discovery

Hold me close and wind me round
Safe in a box of darkness, tight
Held and wrapped so I am sure
I'm back in the earth with Lazarus.

Flesh

1

If I held you round your little neck
And crunched the bones, then I could stop your life.
At other times this pulse and this stuff called skin
Could last out eighty years, eighty plantings
Eighty turns of the world itself.
Sheen, hair, vibration, the warm smell
Whiffle and pantings of life, eye and its apprehending swivel,
Flames its own substance –
Like magnesium dazzle
Like the burning bush unscorched.

All this would go, as the colour off a dead fish wanes,
If I put half an inch of my dead-skin thumb
Or a bit of any matter
Half an inch further in.

2

Little animal, little person
Skin tight across the bone, skin sweating
Eyes stretched and over them, shaped couverture
Little person, little animal.

3

Cat and me are getting old
See where it lies
As if it could not fold its limbs
To keep itself from getting cold.

Old man, old cat sitting together
Waiting; for what?
Something that will drop us both
Beyond the clutch of day and weather.

4 *Moon and flowers*

If there were flowers on the moon
And sharp and bright and eerie that would be
They would be like the laws of nature
Like the light from the stars.

But our flowers are rooted in colour
And they are mortal.

5 *Magnet of the well*

In the clearing stands a well
Round about it pathless woods,
Here, foolishly, the vague rabbit
Lolloped, floppied, ventured out.
Its strange long ears went down and down
Reflected in the black water
Blackness as dazzling as freezing headlamps.
Something pulled it harshly over
And the unrooted light green lace
Of duckweed that should have skimmed the surface
Coated and sank with it, and was dragged down.

Old night

There is a dark river called Chaos,
And it glitters, being thick and dark, with cusps of brilliance
Which make nothing visible.
To its bank even the sunny child
Destined, you'd say, for open meadows, comes.

No river of forgetfulness
Lethe or Acheron or tide that brings
Annihilation where all roll to rest.
No, this is the flood one, the Stirrer
The one that whirls rot, garbage
Suddenly above its banks, throws up
Defilation, broken things.
Equally swept to this littoral, shells
Of uprightness, the beaming surfaces
Of mother-of-pearl success.
Whichever road they were going they arrive at this shore.
Here good comportment stands with smiling face
Nevertheless for virtue come to this ditch.

You are weeping in some smashed place,
A place now used only for getting out of,
All its windows of light shuttered up, bedaubed.
Grit stings and greasy rubbish mires your ankles
As you wait in this sour wreck for shattered buses.
What has happened?
Your idea of your life
Our idea of a town –
Come to this?

Some think they can ride it as the skateboard boys,
Manipulating gravity, shoot out from dark tunnels
Balancing up into daylight on a wave of will
Their lithe persons now nothing but extreme desire.

But not this chariot.

Empedocles said that love comes out of Chaos
Twisting up and then unravelling the rope.
That unsorting the elements, muddling the order, mixing
Gives the momentum from which love leaps, as the spindle
Twirling back up the shaft, winds and unwinds.
But I do not think that love is why the dark glitter
At every turn of beauty pulls us down:
As blood threads flesh this wild and greedy dark
Veins existence.   Fighting the elements
Is what has made us human, and doing so kills us.

Some would say:
Ride the rails then, swing and catch the trapeze bars,
Jump on the bumping cars, run off, twist the handles
To crash into the next, leap off laughing
And dodge the lumbering furies;
Like the graceful ne'er-do-wells who cavort and slap
Their boards about on concrete under the walkways,
Leap to the arms of the magnet your iron is set to,
Ride the lurid glitter, the spume of the dark.

By Lake Huron in winter

Day dies on Huron – huge marginless waste.
Last gleams catch crests of ice scummed over dunes
That merge with the frozen rubble of the lake.
No earth, no water; ice and the whipping wind.

And as it darkens at the edge of the world,
Up there, up there in clarity of sky
Sun's flash, off metal no doubt, and a golden track
That hangs there a little after the planes have gone.

On devastation bent perhaps they fly –
To bomb a southern city, conflagrate.
Fire, first of the elements, is the fiercest, farthest
Most absolute in destruction;
                     and yet

Earth water air without the aid of fire
Remain forever sterile. The atom of carbon
Chained in the leaf awaits the flash from the sun
To set it going and make the rabbit run.

Jenny Joseph was first published by John Lehmann in the 1950s. Her first book of poems, *The Unlooked-for Season* (1960), won her a Gregory Award, and she won a Cholmondeley Award for her second collection, *Rose in the Afternoon* (1974). Two further collections followed from Secker, *The Thinking Heart* (1978) and *Beyond Descartes* (1983). Her *Selected Poems* was published by Bloodaxe in 1992, drawing on these four books. Her latest collection is *Ghosts and Other Company* (Bloodaxe, 1995).

Her other books include: *Persephone* (Bloodaxe, 1986), winner of the James Tait Black Memorial Prize; *Beached Boats* (Enitharmon Press, 1991), a collaboration with photographer Robert Mitchell; and *Extended Similes* (forthcoming from Bloodaxe). She lives in Gloucestershire.